Read for the Brand

The Marvelous Moose

Illustrations by Roslan Fichtner
Narrated by Melody Meadow Lark

Layout and Design by Andy Grachuk
www.JingotheCat.com

Read for the Brand

The Marvelous Moose
Narrated by Melody Meadow Lark

As Melody Meadow Lark I tell,

of wilderness friends I know so well.

The marvelous moose, quite grand and so tall,

among the deer species, the biggest of all!

Regal and stately, like a king or a queen,

high on a mountain, a moose can be seen.

The moose's long legs help them to move,
through deep snow and marshes; they easily groove.
Moose legs are made for terrain so steep,
there's never a time when a moose needs a jeep.
"Swamp donkey," a nickname, some call the moose.
Though he'd outrun a donkey if you turned one loose.

Moose are surprisingly fast and agile on their extremely long legs. They have been known to run as fast as 37 miles per hour, which places them on the top ten fastest animals list. Even rough terrain doesn't slow them down much.

Since moose are much larger than all other deer,

it's fun to find them out on the frontier.

Their height makes them look like their heads touch the clouds.

Sometimes 7 feet, they stand tall and proud.

One thousand pounds is what they can weigh.

Moose wrestling is not a good game to play.

Bull moose are larger than cows; however, both are considered enormous in the deer family. If you measured a moose's body from head to tail, they are typically between 7 and 10 feet long, with an additional 2 inches for their tail. Size varies according to their habitat and the resources available to them.

Moose are dark brown, sometimes almost black.

So, the winter sun warms them across their long back.

However, in summer, their hair is too hot.

They have to find shade, stand in it a lot.

They mostly love water for cooling off fast.

When they find wetlands, they will not walk past.

Moose become stressed in hot temperatures. Since they have few sweat glands, it makes it harder for them to cool off in hot weather. When the sun is hot during the summer months, moose prefer standing in water to cool off. They thrive best in places with longer winters and cooler climates. Their dense undercoat provides excellent insulation for extreme cold.

Moose are great swimmers, so good in fact,

long-distance swimming for them is no act.

A moose can chew plants underwater and eat

water lilies and pondweeds, a favorite treat.

With strangely shaped nostrils, moose noses have two.

A snorkeling moose is something to view.

Moose are very athletic, including their ability to swim. They love the water and can even dive to river bottoms to munch on vegetation that grows there. It is believed that moose can swim up to 6 miles per hour, a little faster than Olympic swimmers; however, a moose can swim much further than any human.

A moose lives alone more often than not.

Deep in the willows makes a great spot.

If you asked a moose what friend a moose had,

to find friend beaver would make a moose glad.

No other friend can build a great dam,

so a moose loves a beaver, because he can!

Male moose are called bulls, with antlers upon
their big moose heads as they lumber along.
Females are cows, having babies each year.
Sometimes they have twins, and mom keeps them near.
A moose can live to the age 25.
Mucking through water and trees helps them thrive.

Moose hooves are large and split in two parts,
leaving a print that can look like a heart.
Their cloven design helps distribute their weight,
so walking in mud won't make them late.
These hooves also make perfect snowshoes.
When caught in a blizzard, they travel right through.

Moose hooves are cloven, meaning they have two parts. They are also large and broad. This design helps them navigate challenging terrain, including snow and mud. Their hooves also act as natural paddles, perfect for excellent swimming.

A bull moose's antlers are majestically placed
and covered in velvet above his big face.
Antlers can weigh up to 45 pounds.
Great might is needed to haul them around.
You can find moose antlers on trails that you tread,
since every year they fall off their moose head.

The hump that moose wear on top of their backs,
gives strength for the massive heads they must pack.
Made of muscle, this hump helps moose move,
through rough terrain, graceful and smooth.
A dewlap or bell hangs from his chin bone,
to rub on a cow moose and leave his cologne.

If a moose were asked to read an eye chart,

that moose would need glasses before he could start.

Good thing a moose nose makes up for that,

it is quite good at smelling, and that is a fact.

The ears on a moose are excellent too,

hearing things long before they are in view.

Moose have very poor eyesight. Their eye placement on each side of their head limits their forward vision. They make up for this with their excellent hearing and smell. Sometimes, while chewing, they will stop to listen for danger. Their big noses help them find food and sniff out danger.

Now that the marvelous moose you have met,
be sure to remember and never forget;
since wilderness places with moose we share,
both moose and land must be handled with care.

When exploring the mountains, as upward you climb,
you'll spot a great moose, in a matter of time.

Moose are not typically aggressive toward humans, but can be dangerous if they feel threatened, such as a mom protecting her babies. Moose in Wyoming are facing some challenges, including habitat loss and predators. Wolves and bears are the main threats to moose, along with parasites that have also threatened their population. Moose hunts in Wyoming are monitored and managed to care for our moose population.

Deeply inspired by Wyoming's culture and scenery, Mary and Roslan aim to capture the state's independent spirit. They've dedicated themselves to the creative mission of bringing the "Cowboy State" to life through hand drawn, vibrant watercolor illustrations and playful rhymes.